I0896427

ABANDONED
MADISON COUNTY

ABANDONED MADISON COUNTY

DEMISE OF AN INDUSTRIAL REGION

DAVID HUMPHREY

AMERICA THROUGH TIME®
ADDING COLOR TO AMERICAN HISTORY

America Through Time is an imprint of Fonthill Media LLC
www.through-time.com
office@through-time.com

Published by Arcadia Publishing by arrangement with Fonthill Media LLC
For all general information, please contact Arcadia Publishing:
Telephone: 843-853-2070
Fax: 843-853-0044
E-mail: sales@arcadiapublishing.com
For customer service and orders:
Toll-Free 1-888-313-2665

www.arcadiapublishing.com

First published 2021

Copyright © David Humphrey 2021

ISBN 978-1-63499-308-1

All rights reserved. No part of this publication may be reproduced, stored in a retrieval system or transmitted in any form or by any means, electronic, mechanical, photocopying, recording or otherwise, without prior permission in writing from Fonthill Media LLC

Typeset in Trade Gothic
Printed and bound in England

CONTENTS

INTRODUCTION

For decades, Anderson, Indiana, was known as a General Motors town, where nearly anyone and everyone could find a job on the production line. Workers were not only guaranteed good wages, but a secure place of employment until retirement age. But through the years, members of the United Auto Workers clashed with corporate owners over benefits and pay. Ultimately, General Motors closed its auto plants in Anderson and relocated to other regions of the world. Had it not been for union and corporate greed, future generations could have found sound employment at Anderson's General Motors plants.

The loss of 22,000 auto manufacturing jobs in Anderson helped lead to the demise of the once prosperous city. In 1970, the city's population was estimated at 70,000 residents. By 2018, that number dropped to 55,000. During this time span, Madison County's population fell from 138,000 to 129,000.

It is no secret that Anderson's economic downfall effected low income families the most. On the city's west side, there are no grocery stores, leaving residents from the area to buy goods at local convenience stores. With no means of transportation to travel to supermarkets across town, the impoverished have no choice but to purchase milk and bread from corner markets at a preposterous price.

The farming crisis of the 1970s and 1980s took its toll on Indiana farms, including those in Madison County. In 1974, there was an estimated 100,000 farms in Indiana. By 2016, only 57,500 farms remained in the state. *Hoosier Ag* magazine reported that Madison County had 667 farms in operation in 2017, with an annual net cash income of $40,789 per farm. In rural areas of the county, amid beautiful country settings, stand dilapidated barns and farmhouses. To many, these structures are eyesores that need to be razed, while the intrigued might contemplate the history behind them.

There are many people who have dubbed the city of Anderson "Little Flint." Indeed, the General Motors factories are gone and they are not coming back. Parents are sending their children to private and charter schools in droves, which could be the final nail in the coffin for Anderson's public schools. And part time jobs with meager pay are all that employers seem to offer.

The future of Anderson and Madison County does not depend on politicians and lawmakers. Instead, it falls on the shoulders of the people who can either rebuild their communities, or watch them crumble to the ground. To illustrate, the Historic Paramount Theatre in Anderson was once in jeopardy of being torn down. If not for the efforts of the Paramount Heritage Foundation, the theatre would have faced the wrecking ball and become yet another parking lot in downtown Anderson. In January 1995, renovation of the theatre began with a grand reopening on August 19, 1995.

A second historic Anderson landmark saved from destruction is the Carnegie Library. After sitting idle for nine years, Project Manager Jim Abraham set out to restore the beloved building. With a budget of $2 million and an eighteen-month time frame, Abraham transformed the historic structure back to its original wonder. The reopening and dedication took place on May 10, 1998. Today, the Carnegie Library building is home to the Anderson Museum of Art.

Renovation of the Carnegie Library and the Historic Paramount Theatre are proof that you can take something old and make it new again. In Alexandria, an abandoned church has become home to the Alexandria Commons Theatre, while the 1897 built Elwood Opera House was renovated into one of the finest venues in Madison County for weddings, class reunions, and luncheons. The old Chesterfield Elementary School is now the site of the Millcreek Civic Center that hosts banquets, high school proms, and youth sports programs. Rather than construct tedious, modern day buildings, why not transform an old farmhouse into a bed and breakfast, or a barn into a dance or music hall.

Our country was founded through compromise, a word that has all but been eradicated from the English language. Members of Generation Y catch plenty of heat from Baby Boomers, who feel that these youngsters are on permanent vacations. Hopefully, this generation will surprise us all, resurrect the word compromise, and serve those individuals who label Anderson "Little Flint" a nice slice of humble pie.

Sadly, general interest in history has fallen to the wayside. Our society lives in a now moment, with little or no interest in what might happen tomorrow, and certainly no interest in what occurred yesterday. There is a story behind every abandoned factory, dilapidated farmhouse, or empty school in Madison County. The curious minded opens doors to these structures and ponders who might have worked there, taught there, or died there. In order for us to move ahead as a society, we must first take a look at where we have been.

1

SCHOOLS OF YESTERYEAR

Old buildings, schools of yesteryear included, are often dealt by society with the same lack of compassion we treat the elderly. Once a person grows old and decrepit, they are shunned by family and friends, placed in nursing homes, out of sight, out of mind. Comparable to the elderly are old school buildings in Madison County. Once age sets in, these schools are either torn down or neglected, until they crumble to the ground. I received my education in Anderson's public schools, and, indeed, it was a good education. But three of the four schools I attended are gone: Roosevelt Elementary School, Madison Heights Junior High, and Madison Heights High School. The fourth, Southview Elementary, is now the site of a preschool. My father, the history buff, collected bricks from schools in the county after being razed, labeling each brick with name and location of the school. Madison Heights High School, Columbia Elementary, Durbin Elementary, and the old Frankton High School to name a few.

Barely visible in a wooded area on County Road East 400 North is the old College Corner School. The one-room schoolhouse was built in 1884 and remained opened until 1920.

An old chalk board at College Corner School.

Above: In 1950, College Corner School opened its new building and educated students until 2005. The structure is located across the street from the first College Corner School on the outskirts of Anderson.

Right: Playground equipment on the grounds of College Corner School.

North Anderson Elementary School opened its doors to students in 1939 and closed in 2005. The empty school is located at 112 Vineyard Street.

Anderson Community Schools Corporation closed six elementary schools in 1982 including Lindberg Elementary. Vandals have broken windows and painted graffiti at the school located on Lindberg Road.

Empty football bleachers at North Side Junior High School in Anderson. The school opened in 1967 and was converted into an Intermediate School in 2010. The latter stayed opened until 2013.

A lone basketball court at the former site of North Side Junior High School.

The former Jackson Township District School #7, located at West Eighth Street Road and County Road North 600 West near Anderson.

Fairview/Summers School is a one-room schoolhouse erected in 1887. The abandoned structure stands in a remote area on the corner of County Roads 200 West and 900 North in Monroe Township.

Right: Keller School was built in 1888 and stands at the intersection of County Roads 300 West and 500 North in Anderson.

Below: On County Road 1800 North in Summittville is a one-room schoolhouse known as White Hall School.

Washington Elementary on South A Street in Elwood opened in 1894 and is currently being renovated into a place of business.

Markleville High School was the home of the Arabians from 1913 through 1969. The last graduating class had fifty-three students.

2

RURAL SCENES

When I was growing up, my family spent many a weekend visiting relatives, several of which lived in rural Madison County. One of those relatives was my uncle, Vick, who owned a farm near Perkinsville. Uncle Vick was easy going, friendly, and far from serious. He reminded me a great deal of comedian Dick Martin. On Uncle Vick's farm, I would help feed the cows and pigs, and play with his dog, Tuscon. I always thought that the drive to the farm seemed an eternity, but later in life, I realized it was nothing more than a 7-mile trip. Our landmark to turn on the country road that led to Uncle Vick's place was a farm owned by Walter Storm. Once I saw Storm's farmhouse, I knew we were minutes away from our destination. Uncle Vick is gone, but his farmhouse and barn remain. Not so for Walter Storm's property. The house and barn were razed many years ago, which once served as my treasured landmark to Uncle Vick's farm.

A Santa Fe train engine sits idle on tracks in Emporia in south Madison County.

This Grand Funk Western Railroad Caboose can be found on abandoned tracks just south of Lapel.

The longest pony truss remaining in the state of Indiana is located on County Road 600 South near Ovid. Built in 1916 and bypassed in 1997, the pony truss is over Fall Creek that runs through south Madison County.

Snowfall, a dilapidated barn, and early morning fog augment this winter scene.

No longer in use is this stone quarry loading station on County Road 650 West in Pendleton. Gravel from an adjacent pit was loaded on to New York Central Railroad cars that traveled to a filling station over a one-mile stretch spur line.

Standing in a field on West Fall Creek Drive in Pendleton is the Fall Creek Service Bridge. Massillon Bridge Company of Massillon, Ohio, built the 100-foot-long wrought-iron bridge in 1884.

A dilapidated barn stands on the outskirts of Pendleton.

Scenic two-story barn near Markleville on State Road 38.

Abandoned homes are a rarity in Pendleton. An exception is this two-story farmhouse located on State Road 67.

In a wooded area on Ridge Road in Anderson is this barely visible "KEEP OUT" sign.

Fugate's Collision Repair located between Anderson and Pendleton is closed, but the American flag on the porch remains.

Left: Rusted dinner bell on abandoned rural property in Pendleton.

Below: Sunlight and blue skies enhance the beauty of this red barn located on a hillside in south Madison County.

This beautifully maintained barn with painted advertisement for Mail Pouch Tobacco is located on State Road 32 between Anderson and Lapel.

Left: A rusted silo stands behind the remains of a demolished barn in south Madison County.

Below: Empty farm structures in a field near Chesterfield.

3

TOWNS OF MADISON COUNTY

Ice cream shops, diners, and basketball courts. Children riding bicycles, teenagers tossing Frisbees, and family picnics at local parks. All are day to day occurrences in the towns of Madison County. Pendleton Historic District, downtown Elwood, and the Chesterfield Spiritualist Camp are all listed on the National Register of Historic Places. Committees comprised of volunteers make a gallant effort to keep the history of these locations alive, for future generations to enjoy. The same could not be said for the town of Alexandria. In 2013, seven buildings in the downtown area were razed, much to the distaste of then-mayor Jack Woods. Though the buildings were built in the late 1800s, and considered historic by Woods, signs of decay threatened public safety. Thus, a former gas station, a dry cleaning business, and five other structures were demolished. Mayor Woods pledged to save other historic buildings in need of renovation, and to keep the town of Alexandria moving ahead in a positive direction.

The Pennsylvania Railroad passenger and freight depot in Frankton was built in 1892. The depot stands on Lafayette Street, between Plum and Mulberry streets, and ceased operation in the mid-1970s.

Grovelawn Cemetery in Pendleton is one of the largest burial grounds for early settlers in Madison County, with a headstone dating back to 1834. Names of the deceased on a gold plate affixed to this padlocked mausoleum are not legible. Grovelawn Cemetery is also known as Pendleton Cemetery or Old Falls Cemetery.

From 1941 through 1967, Armscamp Speedway in Alexandria was the cornerstone on the Indiana short track racing circuit. Joe Armstrong and Frank Scampmort of Anderson were original owners of the track located off Indiana 28. The speedway gained popularity in the 1950s under new owner Paul "Whitey" Karnes, who made vast improvements to the track. All that is left of Armscamp Speedway is the brush covered retaining wall and remnants of the backstretch.

Elwood Airport opened in 1946 and closed in 2008. Hangars on the property still exist as does the famous Fly-In Drive-In Restaurant.

At the end of 2019, KMart stores in Indiana were obsolete including locations in Anderson and Elwood. The KMart store in Elwood began its liquidation sale in mid-September and closed shortly before Christmas.

Built at a cost of $30,000, the Carnegie Public Library in Elwood was one of 164 Indiana public libraries funded by Andrew Carnegie. Once considered a "Marvel of Beauty," the Carnegie Public Library served the Elwood community from 1903 through 1997. The vacated building on North 16th Street was purchased in 2017 but remains empty.

In 1976, the Penn Central Duck Creek Bridge in Elwood was abandoned. The deck plate girder bridge played an important role in a heavy duty branch Pennsylvania Railroad line that featured many passenger trains.

Left: Empty chairs sit outside this abandoned garage in Elwood.

Below: One time site of Jones Speed Shop in Alexandria.

The Sunflower Hotel at Camp Chesterfield was built in 1914 at a cost of $6,887.90. The hotel is now closed but the Friends of Camp Chesterfield Foundation are in the process of raising funds to restore the Sunflower to its original glory.

One of the oldest brick houses in Madison County was built by Allen Cole in 1830. The house is located on Lamb Lane in Perkinsville.

Brockway Golf Club in Lapel opened for play in 1960 and closed in 2011. Longtime professional golfer and greens keeper Kent Williams retired in 2010, after overseeing the nine-hole course for forty-one years. Brockway Golf Club was home course to the Lapel High School boys' golf team.

Entrance to the Aladdin Mantle Lamp Company in Alexandria that closed in 1952.

At the end of 2014, First United Methodist Church in Alexandria closed after losing 80 percent of its congregation. Many blame the closing on the firing of choir director Adam Fraley, an openly gay man. The abandoned church stands at 116 West Broadway Street.

A snow-covered statue of Christ stands alone in a field on the north side of Pendleton. Several other Biblical statues are displayed in the area once used as a religious retreat.

Gaar's Nursery in Chesterfield opened in the mid-1960s and closed in the early 2000s. The main building of the nursery and greenhouses have weathered with time.

An abandoned home in Markleville has become somewhat legendary due to this sign posted on the property. Dozens of vehicles, trailers, and debris fill the lot off State Road 109.

On Main Street in Markleville is the Oliver Farm Equipment Company, which was in operation from 1929 through 1960.

This and next two pages: Abandoned Banner Rock Company in Alexandria founded by C. C. Hall in 1906. Hall sold the rock wool plant in 1929 to Johns-Manville Corporation.

MY
HEART
IS A STRENGTH,
NOT A
LIABILITY

Murals grace the walls of abandoned buildings in downtown Alexandria including this apartment complex on Harrison Street.

A concoction of painted advertisements on the old Democrat Headquarters establishment in Elwood.

Signs decorate a shed on this Summitville property.

Retro gasoline pumps at an abandoned service station in downtown Summitville.

A brick building in Summitville has succumbed with time.

Nearly hidden in a wooded area in Summitville is a tarnished advertisement sign for the Branch Sand and Gravel Company.

Kutche Chevrolet in Elwood closed in the fall of 2014, after twenty-nine years of business. The auto dealership owned by Jerry Kutche sold General Motors products. The vacated building stands on the corner of Indiana 13 and 900 West.

A vacated building on South C Street in Elwood has been the site of several businesses. Most notably, the New Process Laundry and Dry Cleaners founded in 1924 by R. H. Stephens.

Just off the railroad tracks on South 18th Street in Elwood is this abandoned depot-style building.

Caretaker's empty shed at Grovelawn Cemetery in Pendleton.

Right: Retro television set outside the abandoned Ultimate Tan in Alexandria.

Below: Expressions Photography Studio sits empty on Washington Street in Alexandria. The photography studio was once owned and operated by award winning photographer Nancy Wood.

4

ANDERSON

What led to the economic and cultural collapse of Anderson could be debated until the end of time. Opinions may vary on who is responsible for the fall, depending on what side of the fence you stand. Since it was incorporated as a city in 1865, Anderson has been labeled "The Pittsburgh on White River," "Queen City of the Gas Belt," "Puncture Proof City," and, in recent years "Little Flint." For decades, residents of Anderson depended on General Motors as a source of income, with over 20,000 employed at the factories in the 1970s. Apparently, no one took the idiom "Don't put all your eggs in one basket" seriously, and were not prepared for the deindustrialization of the city and the outcome. But when you are a youngster learning to ride a bicycle, and fall off, you either brush yourself and get back on the bicycle or lie on the ground until someone picks you up.

Right: Built in 1961, the Wigwam was home to the Anderson Indians basketball team and hosted the legendary Anderson Basketball Sectional. The 9,000-seat field house closed in 2011.

Below: Anderson's Athletic Park Pool was designed by engineer Walter Bintz, who gained national recognition for his above-ground, egg-shaped swimming pools. Opening in 1925, it served as the city's municipal swimming pool until it closed in 2007. Indiana Landmarks, an Indiana preservation group, placed Athletic Pool on its 10 most endangered list in 2013.

Harvest Supermarket on Cross Street closed in 2016, followed by a second store closing on Columbus Avenue. Currently, five Harvest Supermarkets remain in Madison County. Looming in the background of the Harvest Supermarkets sign is an Anderson water tower. Harvest Supermarkets was founded by the Larry Vores family in 1976.

In April 2017, Marsh announced that they were closing eight Indiana grocery stores, four of which were located in Madison County. One of the Marsh stores to close in Anderson was at 2810 Nichol Avenue on the city's west side. Marsh also closed a second Anderson store on North Broadway, plus stores in Pendleton and Elwood. Local businessmen have recently shown interest in purchasing the Marsh building on Nichol Avenue.

Beginning in 1967, Weidner Chevrolet sold automobiles from this location on North Broadway. After the company went out of business in 2007, Myers Auto World acquired the property before opening a new dealership on Scatterfield Road.

The former Delco-Remy Engineering and Research Center located at the site of Plant 18, opened in 1962 and became Delphi Automotive in May 1994. The colorful landmark on Scatterfield Road shut down in the early 2000s.

Lincolnshire Apartments on West 12th Street was built in 1927 and is currently for sale. No tenants live in the abandoned apartment complex.

Delaware Court Apartments was built in 1929 and closed in 2013 after a fire. Investors are hoping to renovate and reopen the apartment building located on West 10th Street near downtown Anderson.

One of the more popular summer clubs in Anderson was the Dolphin Club. Established in 1966 on East Lindbergh Road, the private club featured an Olympic-style nine-lane swimming pool, clubhouse, tennis and basketball courts, hot tub, sauna, and picnic area. In March 2018, the club filed for Chapter 7 bankruptcy, and sold at an auction the following August for $134,000. As of today, no one has shown interest in purchasing the property.

From its opening in 1930 until it closed in 2008, the State Theatre showed movies and offered live entertainment. After many failed attempts by different owners to renovate and reopen the beloved movie theatre, the city of Anderson purchased the building in 2017 for $127,500 from a California based company. However, it remains an empty historic building.

The Mounds Mall Cinema I–II opened in 1974 with a ribbon cutting by Anderson Mayor Robert Rock. At the gala premiere, Cinema I featured *Pippi in the South Seas* with *Thunderbolt and Lightfoot* shown at Cinema II. The once popular theatre sits on the grounds of the former Mounds Mall and showed its last movies in the 1990s.

For many years, Odell Photographers and Camera Shop sold camera equipment to professionals and amateurs alike, and offered top-quality studio photography to Anderson area clients. Odell's closed its doors in the early 2000s.

Mounds Mall was the first fully enclosed shopping mall founded by Simon Property Group. Located at 2109 South Scatterfield Road, the mall officially opened in April 1965. Woolworth, Zales, and Kroger were among the original tenants. After struggling financially for years, Mounds Mall closed its doors on April 1, 2018.

Above: Factory workers in Anderson found recreation at local bowling alleys, which offered a variety of night leagues. At one time, there were several bowling alleys in the city including East Side Lanes near 10th Street. When the factories left town, the popularity of bowling declined and the facilities eventually closed. Cooper's Championship Lanes is the only Anderson bowling alley to remain open.

Right: Employees at Guide Lamp had several bars to frequent including Miller's Bar at 1228 W. 29th Street. The bar was named after Ronald P. Miller, who owned and operated the business for over thirty years. Miller passed away in 2002, which led to the closing of the facility.

Across town was the Three Pigs Tavern and Restaurant. The closed tavern on East 29th Street in Anderson was a popular watering hole for Delco-Remy workers.

Opposite page: Pennsylvania Railroad once used this deck plate girder bridge, taking passengers from Cincinnati to Logansport, and on to its final destination in Chicago. The abandoned bridge stands over White River near Grand Avenue.

The Delaware Street Bridge was built in 1904 by the Indiana Bridge Co. of Muncie, Indiana. Measuring 630 feet in length, the bridge passed over White River on the north side of Anderson. Nicknamed "The Singing Bridge" for the sound created when tires went over the grate flooring of the span. The bridge was closed in 1980 when county and state officials marked it unsafe.

Railroad tracks run parallel to the Howe Fire Apparatus building. The company closed in 1972.

At one time, service stations were a dime a dozen in Madison County but have grown obsolete over time. Self-serve gasoline pumps and the advancement of automobile technology helped put an end to the corner filling station and old school mechanics. This auto repair shop on North Broadway closed in 2019.

A 1970s-style Ford Thunderbird sits on the grounds of the now closed E-Z Muffler and Brake shop on Columbus Avenue.

Sign on the front lawn of a closed motel in north Anderson.

Condemned by the city of Anderson is the Economy Hotel on Scatterfield Road. The hotel was razed shortly after this photograph was taken.

Signs posted on the boarded-up entrance to the closed Target store on Anderson's south side. In November 2015, it was announced that Target would close thirteen of its locations across the United States, including the store in Anderson. Final shopping day for customers was January 31, 2016.

Anderson's Old Navy clothing store opened on March 5, 2001 and closed on March 31, 2011. A spokesperson for the company stated that the Anderson location was not one of their better stores, which led to the closing.

Situated near the Christian Center is the closed Attic Window. For several years, the Attic Window sold clothes and household items to help benefit the Christian Center, a shelter for the homeless.

After serving his country in the U.S. Army, Charlie Newsom became a master electrician and locksmith. He founded and operated Newsom Electric and Locksmith Service, which served greater Anderson for over forty years at 2203 S. Madison Avenue.

Graffiti covers the exterior wall of the vacated Anderson Pal Club building on Oak Street. For several years, the Pal (Police Athletic League) Club offered karate and boxing to area youngsters, many of whom went on to compete in the Golden Gloves Tournament in Indianapolis.

Vandals spray painted a message at the obsolete May's Park that once offered ice skating and tennis to Anderson residents. Local entrepreneurs have shown interest to revitalize the business.

Message board in the vacated parking lot of the former Guide Lamp factory.

AC Diagnostic Tune-Up Center sits among several discarded automobile parts in a vacated building on the west side of the city.

Spray painted image of a man with the words “God Will Rise” inscribed on it.

Graffiti on a fence behind a brick building falling to the ground.

One of Anderson's first Gas Boom industries was Arcade File. Incorporated in 1892, Arcade File operated until 1900, when it became part of the Nicholson File Company. Located at 34th and East Lynn Streets, Nicholson File produced 5,000 files a day, making it the world's largest producer of files. Nicholson File closed on August 31, 1978 and the structure was razed in 2013. All that remains is the plant's smokestack that has become a landmark on Anderson's east side.

Office building for the DeTamble Motor Car Company in Anderson from 1908 through 1913. The company closed due to financial difficulties. Manufacturing took place in a building immediately behind the office building that later became the Anderson Mattress Company.

Lavelle Foundry was owned and operated by brothers Paul, Tom, and Bernard Lavelle. Located at 1209 East 23rd Street in Anderson, the facility was erected in 1921 and opened for business in 1924. Workers at the foundry produced metal castings for over fifty years. The foundry closed in July 1975. The Lavelle brothers are laid to rest at Anderson's Maplewood Cemetery.

This abandoned structure on East 32nd Street in Anderson once served as a transfer station by trucking companies. Years ago, trucking companies were limited to territories where they could operate, which led to the erection of transfer stations. This allowed the transfer of goods from one carrier to another. Today, interstate commerce has eliminated the need for transfer stations.

The windows and front entrance to the Columbus Avenue Nazarene Church have been boarded up for several years. The church was erected in 1952.

Broken windows at the abandoned Resurrection Ministries near the downtown area.

In 1962, there were 169 nuclear fallout shelters in Madison County, which remained active until the early 1980s. After the Cold War came to an end in 1991, many of the buildings in Madison County with fallout shelters were sold or torn down. But a few remain, including this fallout shelter located near downtown Anderson.

A 5-gallon canister of water and container of crackers discovered inside the fallout shelter.

Untenanted apartment building on the city's west side.

Chairs lean against the exterior wall of this closed club near Arrow Avenue.

For many years, Little League and Babe Ruth gave Anderson youngsters the opportunity to play organized baseball. Over the course of time, Anderson's youth gained more interest in playing football and basketball than they did America's Pastime. The vacated Babe Ruth diamond is on West 25th Street. The empty dugout sits on the grounds of the former Cal Ripken League in north Anderson.

Abandoned garage near the downtown area.

Home for sale by owner on Meridian Street.

Poverty and online banking led to the closing of several banks in Madison County, including this PNC Bank on North Broadway. In 2013, PNC Bank had twenty-one locations in Madison County. Today, that number has dwindled to five.

On Main Street is a deserted building that once housed the Jamz nightclub. Previously, the structure was the site of the San Francisco Inn and the Interurban.

Killbuck Golf Course opened in 1965 and was designed by William Diddel. The eighteen-hole course ran adjacent to Killbuck Park that offered amusement rides, miniature golf, and a picnic area to families. Originally, only General Motors employees could play at Killbuck, but it later became a public course. Though Killbuck was a popular course for Anderson area golfers, owners abruptly closed the business in the fall of 2018.

Shepherd Park on Rangeline Road with netless tennis courts in the background.

Existing bridge support from the old 10th Street Bridge.

Lone silo on the grounds of demolished Delco-Remy plant near Columbus Avenue.

Right: Office entrance to the closed Prime Battery business on West 8th Street.

Below: Cabooses were used on every freight train in the United States until the 1980s. Railroad safety technology during this time led to the reduction of crews, which phased out the caboose car. This Conrail transfer caboose can be found off South Main Street.

An old semi-trailer and spray painted logs sit at the site of a closed tree-cutting business.

For sale are the grounds of the former Pilgrim Holiness Church Camp and Conference Center.

Weeds grow on the property of McClain's Historical Military Armor Museum that closed in 2018. The museum once housed military vehicles and uniforms.

Gene Phillips owned and operated his photography business from this building on West 11th Street. Phillips was a well-established photographer who always had his Chevy El Camino parked outside his studio.

Faded advertisement on a concrete wall for the old Pizza Hut Restaurant on Mounds Road.

The Rider-Lewis Motor Car Company and the Nyberg Automobile Company operated from this site at West Second and Sycamore Streets. The brick factory was built at a cost of $35,000 and went into operation in the fall of 1909. Rider-Lewis almost immediately faced financial trouble. The company was purchased by Henry Nyberg for $40,000 and renamed Nyberg Automobile Company.

McMahan & Leib opened in the early 1900s and merged with Allied Grocers in 1982. Second Harvest Food Bank took over the building on Meridian around 1993. Today, the structure is vacant.

A basketball goal stands on the grounds of the former Wilson's Boys' and Girls' Club. The facility was earlier the site of Hazelwood Elementary School that closed in the early 2000s.

Originally built as an aircraft assembly plant by Anderson Aircraft of North Anderson around 1915. The structure was later home to the Frazer Stove Works, followed by the Anderson Stove Company.

Above and opposite: One time site of the American Strawboard Industries plant, makers of wood and paper products. Over the years, it had many other uses, mainly as a warehouse for storage.

Ivy on abandoned brick home near Shadyside Park.

A quaint abandoned home on Alexandria Pike.

5

RUSTED RELICS

Attending antique car shows has been a favorite summer pastime of mine for several years. Nearly every Madison County town has a car show of its own during the summer months, showcasing some of the finest antique cars in the area. One of my favorite shows is the annual "Goodstock" in Anderson, which highlights cars and music from the 1960s—and some delicious ice cream. Across the county road from where "Goodstock" occurs every June is a wooded area littered with rusted relics; a car graveyard where Chevy Camaros, Ford Mustangs, Volkswagens, and GTOs have been put to rest. Though antique cars in pristine condition are delightful to see, rusted relics abandoned alongside the road or in a field are a photographer's dream.

This bus was once part of the Anderson Transit System. On the rear of the bus are mascots from the city's one time high schools. Madison Heights Pirates, Highland Scots, and the Anderson Indians.

Detailed shot of the Carpenter bus front that once served residents from the city of Anderson.

Foliage covers two abandoned cars located in a field on the south side of Anderson on State Road 67.

Above: This out-of-commission Ford station wagon sits on an empty lot in Perkinsville. On the front of the vehicle is a Route 66 plate.

Right: Detailed shot of the grill from a 1936 Chevrolet truck in the business district of Chesterfield.

A GMC tow truck surrounded by trees and brush on the west side of Anderson.

Rear angle shot of an early model Ford Thunderbird near Anderson.

A rusted Nash automobile with tires in the background located on the grounds of a scrap business in Anderson.

Detailed shot of the Nash name plate.

A delivery truck from the old Alibi Restaurant once located on West 14th Street in downtown Anderson. The Alibi Restaurant was known for including Kentucky Fried Chicken on its menu.